THE
UNITED STATES
SUPREME COURT

Fact, Evidence and Law

Steven R. Schlesinger

UNIVERSITY
PRESS OF
AMERICA

LANHAM • NEW YORK • LONDON

Copyright © 1983 by

University Press of America,™ Inc.

4720 Boston Way
Lanham, MD 20706

3 Henrietta Street
London WC2E 8LU England

Library of Congress Cataloging in Publication Data

Schlesinger, Steven R.
    The United States Supreme Court.

    Includes bibliographical references.
    1. United States. Supreme Court. 2. Judicial
process--United States. II. Title.
KF 8748.S26   1983   347.73'26   83-3648
ISBN 0-8191-3154-7   347.30735
ISBN 0-8191-3155-5 (pbk.)

TO MADELINE AND MARC

Acknowledgments

I would like to thank the Earhart Foundation for a research grant which supported the research and writing of this monograph as well as The American Spectator for permission to reprint material previously published in that journal: Schlesinger and Wilson, The Supreme Court: Fact-free Justice, 12 The American Spectator 18 (1979) (Copyright 1979, The American Spectator). The author is grateful to Francis J. Jones for his fine research and help at all stages of the project and to Madeline Nesse for her constructive and valuable criticisms of several drafts of this monograph. Finally, I thank Janis Allison for her careful research and my colleague, David Nichols, for his helpful suggestions concerning a portion of the manuscript.

Table of Contents

I. Introduction

Legal scholars and other observers of the United States Supreme Court agree that, whatever else it has done, the High Court in the past twenty-five years has been a major policy-maker in the United States.[1] As Professor Martin Shapiro has pointed out, the Supreme Court has initiated at least five major policies: school desegregation, reapportionment, reform of the criminal justice system, basic modifications in federal and state obscenity laws, and the opening up of birth control and abortion services to millions of poor and working-class women. In addition to these major policy formulations, there have been dozens of other, smaller policy changes that have had a substantial impact on American life.[2] This is not to suggest that the Supreme Court's only role in American politics is to make public policy; rather, the Court's policy-making represents a consequence of its responsibility to interpret the Constitution and the laws. It does suggest, however, that policy-making is an important element in the Court's work.

Social scientists agree on very little, but they do generally share the view that proper policy-making can be carried out only when policy-makers take into account the facts, evidence and applicable law relevant to the policies they are formulating.[3] Indeed, one of the criteria by which we evaluate almost all political decisions is the extent to which they accord with the relevant factual and

1

evidentiary background. For example, Congress and state legislatures are expected to use the information gathered in investigations and hearings in formulating legislation.[4] Because Supreme Court Justices play a fundamental role in formulating American public policy, they too should take into account the facts, evidence, and applicable law which are relevant to the questions before them.

This study is intended to show that, in a significant number of the Court's important decisions, including landmark cases in four of the five subject areas noted by Professor Shapiro, the Justices have made serious errors in dealing with the central facts, evidence, and applicable law available to them in each case. In other words, they have made errors concerning some of the most basic constitutive elements in the cases reaching them. The four types of errors made by the Court to be discussed here relate to: 1) the specific facts of the case at bar; 2) the general historical or legal background of the issue under consideration; 3) the meaning of relevant statutes; and 4) the social science or empirical evidence on the issue at bar. These four types of errors have at least one element in common: the commission of each type of error by the Supreme Court reduces the ability of the Court to engage in proper policy-making.

A few brief examples of the Court's errors, examples in which the Court majority does violence to the facts, evidence, or applicable law, are illustrative. Chief Justice Warren's argument in *Reynolds v. Sims*[5] for equal population districting in both houses of state legislatures is premised in part on a factually erroneous statement of the extent of equal population districting in American political history and in contemporary politics[6] (error 2). Justice Clark's argument in *Mapp v. Ohio*[7] for application of the exclusionary rule to state search and seizure cases is premised in part on unwarranted assumptions concerning the deterrent effect on police of that rule[8] (error 4). Justice Brennan's decision concerning the use of racial quotas in *United Steelworkers of America v. Weber*[9] is premised on an erroneous construction of Title VII of the Civil Rights Act of 1964[10] (error 3). Justice Powell's decision in *Village of Arlington Heights v. Metropolitan*

Housing Development Corporation[11] concerning a local zoning decision which was alleged to be racially discriminatory disregarded or ignored important evidence of an official decision-maker's awareness of the racial hostility of his constituents.[12] Finally, Justice Powell's argument in *Gertz v. Robert Welch, Inc.*[13] concerning application of the negligence rule in libel cases is premised on a fear of uncontrolled damage awards for which there is no empirical documentation; in fact, what evidence there is tends to confirm the view that American courts have supervised libel awards rather closely[14] (error 4). All of these errors were determinative of or had a major impact on the Court's decisions in these cases and will be discussed in detail in a later section of this study.

Some readers will be surprised at the extent of the errors of the Court; this surprise will be based on a certain degree of reverence or at least respect for the Court. It is most important, however, that the readers keep an open mind as to the possibility that the Court commits errors of the kinds described. The readers' surprise at the errors of the Court will be reduced when they recognize that, as will become clear from the detailed discussion of the cases, the Justices frequently accuse each other of distorting facts, evidence and law, and that there is some discussion in the professional law review literature about the Court committing the kinds of errors discussed here.

A few words should be said about the means by which the cases discussed in this essay were located. Some were brought to the attention of the author because of secondary literature discussing them and suggesting that the sorts of errors discussed here may have been committed. More important, two research assistants and the author reviewed all Supreme Court decisions for the last thirty years, with a particular eye for those cases in which the dissents suggested the presence of the sorts of errors discussed here. Once a preliminary list of "suspect cases" had been compiled, then such documentary items as lower court decisions, the formal record submitted to the Supreme Court, or congressional debate were consulted in an effort to determine the presence or absence of error. A number of "suspect cases" could not be used because of the absence or ambiguity of documentary evidence bearing on the matter in dispute.

The study will attempt to answer the fundamental question: why should we be so concerned about the Court's errors concerning facts, evidence or applicable law? Why should we care? The basic reason for our concern is that the Court's errors may either contribute to or lead directly to erroneous or incorrect decisions, as would be the case if a legislator ignored or manipulated relevant facts.

The concluding section of the study will put forward some suggestions for preventing or dealing with these errors on the part of the High Court. These include: increased pointing out and criticism of the Supreme Court's errors by scholars, in other words, continuation of the important work of this kind undertaken by such scholars as Alexander Bickel,[15] Henry Hart,[16] Richard Funston[17] and Henry Abraham[18]; an increased level of public awareness and discussion of High Court decisions and especially of the means by which they are reached as opposed to their public policy consequences: this should be led by political leaders, journalists and commentators; serious consideration of at least a gradual overturning of those decisions which are premised on little more than error; scrutiny of nominees for the Supreme Court, directed toward ferreting out individuals whose previous judicial decisions or other writings are characterized by the sorts of errors discussed here; an obligation imposed on the Justices to explain the bases of their factual conclusions; a rule that the principle of *stare decisis* does not apply to factual findings; rules which would encourage or insist that parties file factual briefs and that they file responses to the facts the Court considers; and increased remand of cases for factual development.

This study argues that there is something fundamentally wrong with the means by which the High Court Justices reach some of their decisions, and that there are means by which we should attempt to ameliorate this situation.

II. The Facts of the Case

We now examine a few cases in which the Supreme Court made serious errors relating to the specific facts of the case at bar. Two of these cases revolve around the controversial practice of busing secondary school students for the purpose of achieving a desired racial mix.

Swann v. Charlotte-Mecklenburg Board of Education[19] arose from desegregation orders directed to a large school district covering the Charlotte, North Carolina, metropolitan area. The case, decided in 1971, raised the question whether the ruling in *Brown v. Board of Education of Topeka,*[20] which prohibited *de jure* segregation of students in public schools, required "color-conscious" assignment of students to schools to achieve racial integration and, if so, whether busing to achieve integration was constitutional. The Supreme Court in 1971 made clear, not only that school districts had an obligation to stop using discriminatory practices in the placement of children in schools, but also that they had a positive or affirmative duty to undertake desegregation plans.[21] The Court held that the equal protection clause of the Fourteenth Amendment imposed these obligations.[22] It said that the neighborhood school might have to be partially sacrificed in order to achieve desegregation and recognized for the first time that massive busing would be needed in some places to achieve integration.[23]

In *Swann,* in an opinion by Chief Justice Burger, a unanimous Court ordered that the Charlotte-Mecklenburg Board of Education undertake a massive busing program in order to accomplish the transfer of black students out of formerly segregated black schools and the transfer of white students to previously all black schools. Yet the Court misrepresented the facts when it said that the schools from which blacks were to be bused were segregated by law. As Professor Lino Graglia has pointed out and as the undisputed record submitted to the Supreme Court made clear: "They [the relevant schools] either had been segregated white schools that became heavily black because of the growth of the black population after segregation ended, or had been built in the first place after segregation ended and therefore had never been segregated at all. The justification offered by the Court for what it was doing [ending *de jure* segregation] was simply inapplicable to the facts of the case before it."[24] Thus, a fundamental justification put forth by the Court for this busing rests on a completely erroneous version of the facts.[25] Consequently, the Court, in spite of itself, ordered precisely what it proclaimed in *Swann* to be constitutionally impermissible, namely, busing as a remedy for *de facto,* as opposed to *de jure,* discrimination.

Keyes v. School District No. 1,[26] decided in 1973, was the Supreme Court's first decision on school desegregation in the North, concerning as it did the Denver school district. A federal district court found that the school board, over almost a decade after 1960, had engaged in an unconstitutional policy of deliberate racial segregation with respect to the Park Hill Schools[27]; the court held that the school board had done so by its placement of new schools, by the gerrymandering of school attendance zones, by the use of so-called optional zones, and by excessive use of mobile classroom units, among other means.[28] Park Hill was a neighborhood of eight schools educating at that time less than 38% of Denver's back students and less than 10% of all pupils in the district. Although the core city schools were also segregated in fact, the district court found no segregative policy by the school board as to them.[29]

Justice Brennan, writing for the Court majority, overruled the district court and held that "where plaintiffs prove that the school authorities carried out a systematic program of segregation affecting a substantial portion of the students, schools, teachers and facilities [such as those in Park Hill], [it] is only common sense to conclude that there exists a predicate for a finding of a dual school system [in the district as a whole]" because "racially inspired school board actions have an impact beyond the particular schools that are the subjects of those actions."[30] But Professor Graglia has pointed out and the District Court opinion makes plain[31] whatever the merits of this statement in general, it involves a gross misrepresentation of the facts in Denver. For segregation in core city Denver could not possibly have been the result of segregation in Park Hill, since the core city schools were black or nearly black long before the Park Hill schools became predominantly black.[32] The existence of majority black schools in central Denver was clearly the result not of racial discrimination by the board but of residential patterns.[33] Thus a fundamental rationale for the Court's opinion in *Keyes* collapses because it rests on a regrettable disregard for or misconstruction of the facts. And once again, the Court ordered busing to remedy *de facto* segregation. The impact of the decisions in *Swann* and *Keyes* was substantial: the Court ordered the busing of many children without having found the requisite facts under its own standards.

In *Village of Arlington Heights v. Metropolitan Housing Development Authority*,[34] the Supreme Court held that there was no discrimination violation of the equal protection clause of the Fourteenth Amendment in the failure of a Chicago suburb to rezone an area within its boundaries to permit the erection of multiple-family housing. The Metropolitan Housing Development Corporation (MHDC) contracted to purchase a tract in Arlington Heights in order to build racially integrated low- and moderate-income housing. The contract was contingent on securing rezoning, and MHDC applied to the Village for the necessary rezoning from single-family to multiple-family classification. After the Village denied the rezoning, MHDC and three individual minority respondents filed a suit, alleging that the denial was racially discriminatory and violated the equal protection clause of the Fourteenth Amendment.

The Court's decision in *Arlington Heights* relied heavily upon *Washington v. Davis*[35] which held that official action violates the equal protection clause only when that action is motivated by the intent to discriminate; official action is not unconstitutional simply because it results in a racially disproportionate impact.

In *Arlington Heights,* the Court examined the "sequence of events leading up to the [Village rezoning] decision"[36] to determine if it contained evidence of discriminatory intent on the part of Village officials. Justice Powell said that there was little about that sequence of events to "spark suspicion."[37] He found that the relevant property had been zoned for single-family residences since Arlington Heights first adopted a zoning map, that the rezoning request was treated in accordance with the customary procedures and "suggested that the village plan commission had actually gone out of its way to accommodate MHDC by scheduling three hearings instead of one."[38] But Professor Schwemm argues that these conclusions are misleading:

> The record clearly established that Arlington Heights did not respond to the MHDC proposal as just another rezoning request. Racially explicit letters appeared in the local newspaper,[39] and thousands of residents signed petitions opposing the development. The plan commission held its additional hearings in a high school auditorium to hold the demonstrative overflow crowds, not so much to consider the merits of the MHDC proposal as to accommodate the unprecedented number of homeowners and "civic" group spokesmen who wanted to register their opposition to the development.[40]

Professor Schwemm recognizes that "an official could ignore expressions of racial bias by his constituents and still reach the decision the constituents desired, and courts should not lightly assume otherwise."[41] But he says the Court should not simply have assumed that this is what transpired in this case:

> When the evidence of community racial hostility is strong, however, a rebuttable presumption that this hostility affected the

official decision is appropriate,[42] particularly when one of the decision-makers states, as the Arlington Heights Village president did, that "the objections of the residents is [sic] a mandate to reject this proposal."[43] Hence, Justice Powell's conclusion that the procedural history of the MHDC zoning hearings was not suspicious is simply not consistent with the record in *Arlington Heights.* After *Davis,* the plaintiff in an equal protection case is essentially required to prove a negative—that the challenged decision was not based on any reason other than racial discrimination—and this is difficult enough without the Court ignoring evidence of an official decision-maker's awareness of the racial hostility of his constituents.[44]

It could be argued that the Village president's statement concerning the "objections of the residents" referred to non-racial objections to the housing proposal and, therefore, it gives no indication of discriminatory intent. But this argument is not satisfactory:

> . . . the president's quotation indicates that the Trustees were motivated by the citizens' opposition. This allows us to look at the nature of the citizens' opposition to determine what motivated the Trustees. Since the citizens' opposition was at least partly racial, it seems to me that an inference could be drawn that the Trustees' decision could be considered to be at least partly racially-based.[45]

Professor Schwemm also points out that the Supreme Court's decision in this case recognized that a "partly racially-based" decision might be unconstitutional[46] but decided that there was not even enough evidence in the record to make out a case of such a "partly racially-based" decision by the Village trustees.

In this case, as well as in the *Davis* case, the Court formulated a test for discrimination under which many plaintiffs will clearly have considerable difficulty bearing the necessary burden of proof. In light of this, it is especially important that the Court undertake, as it did not in this case, the fairest and most complete examination of all the evidence.

III. Historical or Legal Background

We now turn our attention to cases in which the Court has made serious errors with regard to the general historical or legal background of the issue under consideration.

In 1964, the Supreme Court decided *Reynolds v. Sims*[47] and its companion cases.[48] In *Reynolds,* the Court took it upon itself to fashion a remedy for the reprehensible disregard shown by the Alabama legislature for the provisions of its state constitution requiring legislative reapportionment every ten years, in accordance with decennial census figures; the Alabama legislature had not been reapportioned since 1911. Virtually abandoning all pretense of ascending from the specific facts of the case before it to the shaping of an appropriate rule, the Court dictated that the Equal Protection Clause of the Fourteenth Amendment requires that both houses of a state legislature—any state legislature—be apportioned on a "one man, one vote" basis, that is, that state legislators must represent equal numbers of people.[49] Then, with a wave of its newly constructed rule, the Court proceeded to declare the legislatures of all the states under review to be unconstitutionally apportioned.[50]

In writing the majority opinion mandating equal population districting, Chief Justice Warren repeatedly asserted the basic premise that "the fundamental principle of representative government in this country is one of equal representation for equal numbers of people . . . ."[51] With this standard serving as their guiding light, the *Reynolds* majority devoted the bulk of their opinion to scouring the constitutional terrain for such qualifying considerations as would justify significant deviation from the equal population standard. It should surprise no one that the Court was unable to discover any such considerations. The Warren Court, following in the great tradition of its predecessors, regarded itself as a bulwark against encroachments on the nature and purpose of republican self-government; and no friend of republican institutions would wish to see "the fundamental principle of representative government" vitiated by substantial exceptions to that principle. The problem with Warren's opinion lies not with the inferences he draws from his basic premise. Rather, the problem lies with the basic premise itself: that premise is patently false.

As Justice Frankfurter had painstakingly shown two years earlier in *Baker v. Carr*[52]:

> However desirable and however desired by some among the great political thinkers and framers of our government, [equal population districting] has never been generally practiced today or in the past. It was not the English system, it was not the colonial system, it was not the system chosen for the national government by the Constitution, it was not the system exclusively or even predominantly practiced by the states at the time of adoption of the fourteenth amendment, it is not predominantly practiced by the states today.[53]

As to the design for the national government contemplated by the Constitution, Chief Justice Warren argues that, due to the compromises made at the Philadelphia Constitutional Convention, the system of representation required of the national government by the Constitution has absolutely no relevance to the state reapportionment discussion.[54] The so-called federal analogy is inapposite, says the Chief Justice, because, whereas "[p]olitical subdivisions of States . . . never were and never have been considered as sovereign entities, . . . at the heart of our constitutional system remains the concept of separate and distinct governmental entities which have delegated some, but not all, of

₁ their formerly held powers to the single national government.''[55] Shades of John C. Calhoun.[56] One would think that the Civil War rendered this argument something less than respectable. Indeed, it is nothing less than incredible to find the states' rights argument being used in the service of a quantum expansion of federal power over the states. ˋ

It is no wonder that Chief Justice Warren, in order to deny the relevance of the national governmental structure to apportionment theory, is willing to resurrect the discredited states' rights philosophy, for this is the only argument which could accomplish that denial. The Chief Justice is willing to go to such lengths to ·deny that the national experience is relevant because to admit otherwise would be to open the door to damning evidence of just how small a role equal population districting plays in the theory of representation underlying the structure of our national institutions. The President is elected through the Electoral College which does not operate according to Chief Justice Warren's principle. The Supreme Court is not even elected, but is appointed by the President and confirmed by the Senate. Representation in the Senate has nothing whatever to do with Chief Justice Warren's principle, and, in the House where districting by population is the general rule, each state is given at least one vote, even though some states are considerably smaller in population than the average congressional district. In sum, how could Chief Justice Warren's principle be fundamental when it has been rejected in the overwhelming number of cases, both at the state and federal levels? So much for "equal representation for equal numbers of people"; the governments of the United States were never intended to be simplistically majoritarian.

Indeed, it is strange to find the Supreme Court, which is by almost any account the least democratic branch of the national government, arguing blindly for a quantitative measure of representative government—an argument which by its very terms would exclude the Court from a legitimate place in the deliberations of that government. And to make matters worse, not only does *Reynolds* remain the law of the land, but its principle of equal population districting has been extended to include all local governments of general jurisdiction.[57]

It could be argued that, when Chief Justice Warren says that "equal representation for equal numbers of people" or "one man, one vote" is a fundamental constitutional principle, he means that this principle as applied would yield the fairest, most democratic, most equal apportionment. But this is clearly not the case. First, through the use of computers, district lines may be drawn so that, while district populations are roughly equal, particular groups of voters—ethnic, racial, urban, etc.—are favored or disfavored.[58] Second, when district populations must be roughly equal, districts may have to be so large that they include serious geographical impediments—mountains, deserts, large bodies of water—to ready access for the constituent to his representative. Indeed, such impediments are discussed in one of the Supreme Court's leading cases on apportionment, *Lucas v. the Forty-fourth General Assembly of Colorado.*[59] Finally, it follows from what Chief Justice Warren says that voters in districts with the largest populations will have the most "diluted," the least desirable or effective representation. However, whether this is the case will depend at least as much on the effectiveness of the particular legislator and on whether the individual voter can associate with the dominant interests in the district as on the size of the district population. After all, a voter from a district with a small population may be in the unenviable position of having an ineffective representative or he may be part of a group to whom the representative does not pay nearly as much attention as it would like, perhaps because it lacks the voting strength which would compel greater attention from the representative.

We now turn to *Roe v. Wade*[60] and *Doe v. Bolton,*[61] both decided in 1973 and generally considered to be among the Burger Court's most controversial decisions. In *Roe* and *Doe*, the Court interpreted the Fourteenth Amendment's due process clause to mean that a state may not enact abortion legislation which regulates abortion (i.e., affects the period of gestation) prior to the time children are said to be viable.[62] A child is "viable" when he or she is able to live outside the mother's womb, with or without artificial assistance.[63] The Court stated that viability is generally at twenty-eight weeks but may occur as early as twenty-four weeks.[64]

In his article on the misguided character of these decisions, Professor Robert M. Byrn[65] has shown that the decisions were based upon factual errors concerning history and concerning the status in law of unborn children. He demonstrates the Court's historical errors by discussing its thoroughly inadequate interpretation of the status of abortion in common law,[66] in nineteenth-century American statutes,[67] and at the time the Fourteenth Amendment was adopted.[68] His article is replete with instances of gross historical oversights, mistakes and distortions committed by the Court majority. For example, the Court maintained in *Roe* that "the few state courts called upon to interpret their laws in the late 19th and early 20th centuries did focus on the State's interest in protecting the woman's health rather than preserving the embryo and fetus."[69] The Court cited only one 1858 New Jersey case[70] as support for this proposition. Professor Byrn, by quoting from relevant judicial decisions in New Jersey, Alabama, Colorado, Iowa and Michigan, reveals the opposite of this statement to be true.[71] Relevant judicial decisions from these states emphasize in explicit terms and do focus on the state's interest in the protection of the unborn.[72] For example, a Colorado court said in 1872 that the state's abortion law was "intended specifically to protect the mother and her unborn child from operations calculated and directed to the destruction of the one and the inevitable injury of the other."[73] An Alabama court said, "[D]oes not the new being . . . acquire a legal and moral status that entitles it to the same protection as that guaranteed to human beings in extrauterine life?"[74]

As to the Supreme Court's misunderstanding of the status in law of unborn children, the Court maintained in *Roe* that "in areas other than criminal abortion, the law has been reluctant to endorse any theory that life, as we recognize it, begins before live birth or to accord legal rights to the unborn except in narrowly defined situations. . . ."[75] But of course, reluctance is not refusal. At any rate, the Court attempted to support this view of the law by discussing briefly actions for prenatal injuries and for stillbirth involving wrongdoing, as well as the property rights of the unborn child.[76] However, William J. Maledon demonstrates clearly that the Court was mistaken: that in the specific areas of law discussed by the Court, an unborn child is indeed a legal person.[77] Maledon shows that the legal life of a human being begins at conception for purposes of the law of property.[78] Maledon speaks of developments in the law of torts which recognize "the right to maintain an action for the wrongful death of a child from prenatal injuries. Where the child is born alive and subsequently dies as a result of injuries received prior to birth, the courts which have considered the question are almost unanimous in allowing the child's estate to bring an action for wrongful death."[79] He concludes generally, after an exhaustive study of the relevant cases, that "in recognizing a cause of action for injury inflicted before birth, the law has recognized the legal interests in personality of the unborn child. . . . If one accepts the trend of modern tort cases he must conclude that Professor Prosser was correct in stating that "the unborn child in the path of an automobile is as much a person as the mother.""[80]

It is sad, indeed, that decisions which control the fate of so many fetuses and which affect one of the most divisive and emotional issues of our day should be based, at least in part, on these errors.

IV. Statutory Construction

We now examine a number of those cases in which the Supreme Court made serious errors concerning the meaning of relevant statutes.

In *Calbeck v. Travelers Insurance Company*,[81] the Supreme Court ruled that a workman injured on navigable waters may obtain compensation under the Federal Longshoremen's and Harbor Workers' Compensation Act although the particular injury might also be within the reach of a state workmen's compensation act.[82]

The case turned on Section 3(a) of the Longshoremen's Act which restricts the Act to disability or death resulting "from an injury occurring upon the navigable waters of the United States . . . if recovery for the disability or death through workmen's compensation proceedings may not validly be provided by state law."[83] The Court's opinion by Justice Brennan pointed out that, prior to passage of the Longshoremen's Act in 1927, the Supreme Court had by a series of decisions denied recovery under state compensation acts to workmen employed on navigable waters because of the United States' exclusive admiralty jurisdiction,[84] but had also permitted such compensation under state laws when the activities giving rise to the disability or death were "maritime but local" or "of local concern."[85] The Court noted that the Longshoremen's Act was passed to obviate the possibility of an injury on navigable waters which would not be covered by any compensation law[86]; therefore, the Court reasoned, the Act should be construed "to ensure that a compensation remedy exist[s] for all injuries sustained by employees on navigable waters, and to avoid uncertainty as to the source, state or federal, of that remedy."[87]

In a vigorous dissent, Justice Stewart, joined by Justice Harlan, attacked the statutory interpretation of the majority:

> In the Longshoremen's and Harbor Workers' Compensation Act, 33 USC Section 901-950, Congress carefully provided for the recovery of benefits only "when recovery for the disability or death through workmen's compensation proceedings may not validly be provided by State law." 33 USC Section 903 (a). Now, 35 years later, the Court concludes that Congress did not really mean what it said. I cannot join in this exercise in judicial legerdemain. I think the statute still means what it says, and what it has always been thought to mean—namely, that there can be no recovery under the Act in cases where the State may constitutionally confer a workmen's compensation remedy. While the result reached today may be a desirable one, it is simply not what the law provides.[88]

In an attempt to circumvent the clear language of the statute, the majority attempts to interpret the congressional intent underlying the Federal Longshoremen's Act as though it were created to provide compensation for all injuries sustained by employees on navigable waters, "whether or not a particular injury might also have been within the constitutional reach of a state workmen's compensation law."[89] To this end, Justice Brennan attempts to document Congress' concern that the coverage of the Longshoremen's Act be broad and that longshoremen be spared the "uncertainty, expense and delay of fighting out litigation whenever their cases fell within or without the state acts. . . ."[90] But his documentation is irrelevant to the issue at hand because the applicable congressional history reveals with complete clarity that the Act was created to remedy a gap where an injured worker could not be provided for under the constitutional reach of state compensation laws and would be left with no remedy whatsoever.

This was spelled out by the Chairman of the Senate Judiciary Subcommittee: "We are proceeding on the theory that these people *cannot* be compensated under the New York Compensation law or any other compensation law."[91] Indeed, Congress repeatedly emphasized that the purpose of the Act was to provide a compensation remedy to those who *could not* obtain such relief under state law:

> If longshoremen could avail themselves of the benefits of State compensation laws, there would be no occasion for this legislation: but, unfortunately, they are excluded from these laws by reason of the character of their employment; and they are not only excluded but the Supreme Court has more than once held that Federal legislation cannot, constitutionally, be enacted that will apply State laws to this occupation.[92]

> The committee . . . recommends that this humanitarian legislation be speedily enacted into law so that this class of workers, practically the only class without the benefit of workmen's compensation, may be afforded this protection. . . .[93]

Justice Stewart in fact noted that, in one of the companion cases decided in *Calbeck,* there had already been an award under the Louisiana act and that in the other case there was a proceeding pending under the Texas act under which an award was clearly allowable.[94]

Congress' intent in this case was clear; the Court should have given effect to that intent.

A telling example of the Court's misinterpretation of congressional intent occurred in *Rosenberg v. Fleuti* [95] which involved the Court's interpretation of the word "entry" as defined in the 1952 Immigration and Naturalization Act.[96]

George Fleuti was a Swiss national who had been originally admitted to the United States for permanent residence on October 9, 1952. He had been in the United States continuously since that time except for a visit to Ensenada, Mexico, in August 1956. In April 1959, the Immigration and Naturalization Service (INS) sought to deport Fleuti, alleging that he had been convicted of a crime involving moral turpitude. In order for the INS to deport

Fleuti, the Act required it to show that he had entered the country some time after December 24, 1956.[97] When the INS's first complaint was dismissed because the crime was a petty offense and not of the magnitude encompassed within the statute, a second action was brought charging Fleuti with a violation of 8 U.S.C. Section 1182 (a) (4): that at the time of the 1956 return he was excludable because he was afflicted with psychopathic personality by reason of the fact that he was a homosexual.[98] Deportation was ordered and Fleuti appealed; that appeal eventually reached the United States Supreme Court.[99]

The Court granted certiorari in order to consider the constitutionality of Section 1182 (a) (4) as applied to Fleuti. Justice Goldberg, for the majority, however, bypassed that issue by stating that the case turned on a threshold issue of statutory interpretation.[100] The real issue to be determined, said Justice Goldberg, is what constitutes "entry" within 8 U.S.C. Section 1101 (a) (13).[101] The Court held that Fleuti's 1956 trip did not include an "entry."

Citing *Ex rel Volpe v. Smith,*[102] the Court stated that the definition of the word "entry" for immigration purposes had evolved judicially, resulting in a rather strict construction of the meaning of entry.[103] The Court concluded that the meaning was so harsh that courts had redefined the word.[104] It was in light of this redefinition, noted Justice Goldberg, that Congress included the definition of entry in the 1952 revision of the immigration laws.[105] Citing the legislative history, Justice Goldberg held that Congress intended the meaning of "entry" to be defined in light of the facts and decisions in the cases in which the courts had redefined the word.

Justice Goldberg was quite correct in saying that Congress intended the meaning of "entry" to be defined in light of the prior cases—but that meaning clearly encompassed Fleuti's trip; the House and Senate Committee Reports preceding the enactment of the bill contained the following paragraph:

> More recently, the courts have departed from the rigidity of that rule and have recognized that an alien does not make an entry upon his return to the United States from a foreign country where he had

no intent to leave the United States (*DiPasquale v. Karnuth,* 153 F.2d 878 (2d Cir. 1947)), or did not leave the country voluntarily (*Delgadillo v. Carmichael,* 332 U.S. 388 (1947)). The bill defines the term entry as precisely as practicable, giving due recognition to the judicial precedents. Thus any coming of an alien from a foreign port or place or an outlying possession into the United States is to be considered an entry, whether voluntary or otherwise, unless the Attorney General is satisfied that the departure of the alien, other than a deportee, from this country was unintentional or was not voluntary.[106]

However, once having reached this conclusion, Justice Goldberg went on to hold that, while Congress has the power to exclude all undesirable aliens, it did not intend to exclude aliens long resident in this country after lawful entry who have "merely stepped across an international border . . . in an innocent, casual and brief manner . . . and who returned in a couple of hours."[107] Justice Goldberg therefore concluded that Fleuti's return from Mexico did not constitute an "entry" and that he could not be deported.[108]

While this result might have been desirable, it is clear from the legislative history that this was not the result intended by Congress. As the previous quotation from the House and Senate report states, Congress intended only to "give recognition to the judicial precedents."[109] In each of the cases cited by the report, the resident alien had either unintentionally or involuntarily left the country. In *Delgadillo,*[110] a merchant marine was taken to a Cuban hospital after his ship had been torpedoed in the Caribbean during World War II, hardly a situation that can be considered voluntary. As for *DiPasquale,*[111] the resident alien boarded an overnight train from Detroit to Buffalo and while he was asleep the train passed through Canada. The Court found that deportation was not warranted because the alien never had knowledge that the train would pass through Canada. In short, none of the cases cited by Congress or by Justice Goldberg in his opinion support the proposition that an entry includes a trip which is taken voluntarily or intentionally.[112]

As for the evidence in this case, Fleuti testified that the purpose of the Mexico visit was just to take a trip. Justice Goldberg's opinion ignores the fact that the judicial precedents relied on by Congress all involved situations in which the alien unintentionally or involuntarily left and then reentered the country. This case is plainly one in which Congress intended that the entry be considered an "entry" for purposes of the statute. As Justice Harlan states in dissent, the majority in this case was not construing the statute, but constructing it.[113]

United Steelworkers of America v. Weber[114] involved the legality, under a Federal anti-discrimination statute, of a special training program provided by the Kaiser Aluminum and Chemical Corporation for its workers at one of its plants. Trainees were selected on the basis of seniority, with the provision that at least 50% were to be black until the percentage of black craft workers was the same as the percentage of blacks in the work force. In 1974, thirteen craft trainees were selected, seven black and six white. The most junior black selected had less seniority than several white workers, one of whom was Weber.[115] Weber brought a class action, complaining that he had been discriminated against in violation of Sections 703(a) and (d) of Title VII of the Civil Rights Act of 1964.[116] These sections, according to *Weber,* prohibited the type of racial quota being used by Kaiser. The Court majority, in an opinion by Justice Brennan, held that Title VII does not prohibit this sort of affirmative action program.[117]

Justice Rehnquist's dissent, joined by Chief Justice Burger, was angry and bitter,[118] but the majority's "interpretation" of Title VII provided much about which to be angry and bitter. As Professor Henry Abraham has observed:

> If words mean anything, the basic statute involved, namely the 1964 Civil Rights Act's Title VII, would indeed seem to be crystal clear in *proscribing* the kind of racial quotas that the United States District Court and the United States Court of Appeals found to have violated Brian Weber's rights, but which, on appeal, the highest court of the land *upheld* in a 5:2 decision.[119]
>
> ... Section 703(a) makes it unlawful for an employer to classify his or her employees "in any way which would deprive or tend to

deprive any individual of employment opportunities or otherwise adversely affect his status as an employee because of such individual's race, color, religion, sex or national origin." And, perhaps even more tellingly, Section 703(j) provides that the Act's language is not to be interpreted "to require any employer . . . to grant preferential treatment to any individual or to any group because of the race . . . of such individual or group."[120]

If the words of the statute were not sufficient to demonstrate the intent of Congress to proscribe racial quotas, one need only review the *Congressional Record* recording the debate that led to the passage of the 1964 Civil Rights Act.

> Thus, the . . . successful Senate floor leader, Senator Hubert Humphrey, in responding to concerns voiced by doubting colleagues, vigorously and consistently gave assurances that no racial quotas or racial workforce statistics would be employable under the law. In one exchange with his colleague, Willis Robertson, he made the following offer: "If the Senator can find in Title VII . . . any language which provides that an employer will have to hire on the basis of percentage or quota related to color . . . I will start eating the pages one after another, because it is not in there." Cong. Rec. 110:7420 (1964)[121]

Justice Brennan's majority opinion downplays the clear language of the statute by pointing to the fact that the quota agreement between the Steelworkers Union and the Kaiser Corporation was not government-required but was voluntary.[122] This argument is unsatisfactory for two reasons: first, the history of the development of affirmative action programs in the United States and at Kaiser Aluminum shows that they are not simply voluntary[123]; as Justice Rehnquist said in his powerful dissent:

> The Office of Federal Contract Compliance (OFCC), subsequently renamed the Office of Federal Contract Compliance Programs (OFCCP), is an arm of the Department of Labor responsible for ensuring compliance by Government contractors with the equal opportunity requirements established by Exec. Order No. 11246. . . .
> Executive Order No. 11246, as amended, requires all applicants for federal contracts to refrain from employment discrimination

and to "take affirmative action to ensure that applicants are employed, and that employees are treated during employment, without regard to their race, color, religion, sex or national origin. . . ."

The affirmative action program . . . for non-construction contractors requires a "utilization" study to determine minority representation in the work force. Goals for hiring and promotion must be set to overcome any "underutilization" found to exist.

The OFCC employs the "power of the purse" to coerce acceptance of its affirmative action plans. Indeed, in this litigation, "the district court found that the 1974 collective bargaining agreement reflected less of a desire on Kaiser's part to train black craft workers than a self-interest in satisfying the OFCC in order to retain lucrative government contracts" 563 F.2d 216, 226 (CA5 1977). . . .[124]

In light of the background and purpose of § 703(j), the irony of invoking the section to justify the result in this case is obvious. The Court's frequent references to the "voluntary" nature of Kaiser's racially discriminatory admission quota bear no relationship to the facts of this case. Kaiser and the Steelworkers acted under pressure from an agency of the Federal Government, the Office of Federal Contract Compliance, which found that minorities were being "underutilized" at Kaiser's plants . . . that is, Kaiser's work force was racially imbalanced. Bowing to that pressure, Kaiser instituted an admissions quota preferring blacks over whites. . . .[125]

Second, whether affirmative action programs are required or voluntary makes no difference in the context of 703(a) which makes no distinction between required and voluntary actions but, rather, proscribes all discriminatory classifications.

Chief Justice Burger's dissent in *Weber* is striking in that he makes clear that the intent of Title VII is perfectly apparent, even to one who disagrees with Congress' decision as to the status of quotas:

> The Court reaches a result I would be inclined to vote for were I a member of Congress considering a proposed amendment to Title VII. I cannot join the Court's judgment, however, because it is contrary to the explicit language of the statute and arrived at by means wholly incompatible with long established principles of separation of powers. Under the guise of "statutory construction,"

the Court effectively rewrites Title VII to achieve what it regards as a desirable result. It "amends" the statute to do precisely what both its sponsors and its opponents agreed the statute was *not* intended to do.[126]

In this case, then, the Court permitted just the sort of quota program Congress intended to proscribe and legitimated the existence of many other similar programs across the country.

V. Social Science Evidence

We now examine a number of cases in which the Court has made serious errors concerning the social science or empirical evidence on the issue at bar.

In 1961, the Court decided *Mapp v. Ohio*[127] by a vote of 6–3. In an effort to apply and enforce the Fourth Amendment search and seizure provisions, the Court decided in that case to extend to state court proceedings what is commonly known as the exclusionary rule—a rule which had been binding on federal courts since 1914.[128] The exclusionary rule is a rule of evidence which excludes, i.e., renders inadmissible in a criminal proceeding, evidence that is illegally obtained by law enforcement officials; it has resulted in the release of literally thousands of dangerous and violent persons.[129] Justice Clark, who claimed that his majority opinion was "founded on reason and truth,"[130] suggested that the rule has a deterrent effect on police—the notion that police will not obtain evidence illegally if they are unable to use it against the defendant in a trial. Justice Clark said, "Only last year the Court itself recognized that the purpose of the exclusionary rule 'is to deter—to compel respect for the constitutional guaranty in the only effectively available way—by removing the incentive to disregard it.' "[131] Despite this strong language about the deterrent impact of the rule suggesting that deterrence of illegal police behavior is the rationale for *Mapp,* Justice Clark claims in *Mapp* that his majority opinion is premised at bottom on protection of individual privacy—insuring that the State will derive no benefit from invasions of individual privacy—rather than the deterrent effect he claims the rule has.[132] However, later Supreme Court cases dealing with the rule, for example, *Linkletter v. Walker* (1965) and *United States v. Calandra* (1974),[133] explicitly assert that imposition of the rule is justified by its deterrent effect on police. Ironically, it is Justice Clark himself who asserts in *Linkletter* that "all of the cases since *Wolf* [this would include *Mapp*] requiring the exclusion of illegal evidence have been based on the necessity for an effective deterrent to illegal police action. . . ."[134]

And yet there was not at the time of *Mapp* nor is there today any substantial evidence, empirical or otherwise, that the rule is an effective deterrent. Justice Clark argued that certain alternatives to the rule have been ineffective,[135] but that argument in no way establishes the deterrent effectiveness of the rule. The reason Justice Clark included no evidence of the deterrent effectiveness of the rule is simply that at that time there was none. In effect, Justice Clark transformed a hypothesis into a statement of fact; when, as in *Mapp,* fundamental matters of law enforcement are at stake, this procedure—making up facts—seems thoroughly inadequate.

Since *Mapp,* a great deal of empirical study has been devoted to the deterrent effect of the rule, and the evidence indicates that the rule is, at best, a weak deterrent. In fact, Justice Powell's majority opinion in the 1976 companion cases of *Stone v. Powell* and *Wolff v. Rice*[136] spoke of the "absence of supporting empirical evidence" for the claim that the rule deters improper police behavior. This is an understatement: six of the seven empirical studies written on the deterrent effectiveness of the exclusionary rule conclude that the rule is not an effective general deterrent.[137] The author of the seventh article comes to no definitive conclusion as to deterrent effectiveness.[138] Indeed, the staunchest defender of the rule in the social science community has recently admitted that "the rule has not always or even often worked [to deter police misconduct]."[139] Oaks' 1970 study of law enforcement in Cincinnati between 1956 and 1967 convinced him that:

As a device for directly deterring illegal searches and seizures by the police, the exclusionary rule is a failure. There is no reason to expect the rule to have any direct effect on the overwhelming majority of police conduct that is not meant to result in prosecutions, and there is hardly any evidence that the rule exerts any deterrent effect on the small fraction of law enforcement directed at prosecution.[140]

Ban's two studies of the impact of the rule in Boston and Cincinnati, conducted in the mid-1960's, also tend to confirm the ineffectiveness of the rule.[141] Ban concludes that the rule showed spotty effectiveness in Boston and almost none in Cincinnati.

Spiotto's study of motions to suppress in Chicago between 1950 and 1971 convinced him that "the deterrent rationale for the rule does not seem to be justified" and that "given the present status of the law and the workings of the exclusionary rule, change is warranted. . . ."[142]

Common sense accords with the conclusions of the empirical studies: the operating scope of the rule is limited to exclude only that evidence presented at trial, and given the frequency of plea bargaining (over 90% of criminal cases in most large American cities) and of police actions aimed at harassment or seizure of contraband and not at prosecution ending in a trial, that operating scope is narrow; the impact of the rule falls only indirectly on the policemen, since disciplinary action is rarely taken against the officer specifically responsible for the illegal seizure of evidence; the impact of the rule's effect is borne by the prosecutor who is not responsible for the illegal seizure and who has virtually no power to prevent or punish police misconduct; officers whose illegal actions result in loss of convictions may still receive the implicit or explicit support of their superiors if their behavior conforms to police group norms; and finally, police effectiveness—and thus promotion, salary, etc.—is judged by the number of arrests which "solve" crimes as far as the police are concerned, and not by the number of resultant convictions. From this it is evident that the deterrent effect of the rule is, at best, indirect. And yet, to this day the decision of the Court in *Mapp* remains the law of the land and has resulted in the release by state court judges of thousands of persons who committed the serious crimes with which they were charged.[143]

Gertz v. Robert Welch, Inc.[144] is one of the Court's recent pronouncements on the law of libel. Justice Powell's majority opinion states that in libel cases involving the news media, the probable adverse effects of libel legislation on the media must be balanced against the individual's right to protect his reputation.[145] One of the possible adverse effects cited by the majority is uncontrolled damage awards levied by juries against the news media[146]:

> The common law of defamation is an oddity of tort law, for it allows recovery of purportedly compensatory damages without evidence of actual loss. Under the traditional rules pertaining to actions for libel, the existence of injury is presumed from the fact of publication. Juries may award substantial sums as compensation for supposed damage to reputation without any proof that such harm actually occurred. The largely uncontrolled discretion of juries to award damages where there is no loss unnecessarily compounds the potential of any system of liability for defamatory falsehood to inhibit the vigorous exercise of First Amendment freedoms. Additionally, the doctrine of presumed [punitive] damages invites juries to punish unpopular opinion rather than to compensate individuals for injury sustained by the publication of a false fact.[147]

The Court held that, in libel suits involving private individuals, it is not sufficient for the plaintiff to show that the statements in question are false: in order to prevail and to collect compensatory damages, he must prove that the broadcaster or publisher was negligent (e.g., had failed to check sources) in disseminating the statements to the public.[148]

Justice White's dissent maintains that, in performing the kind of balancing which the majority claims is necessary, the Court has badly overweighted the claims of the press.[149] He points out that the majority's fears of uncontrolled damage awards by juries and of a press made timid by fear of large libel awards have no factual or empirical basis, because the majority fails to consider the common sense of most jurors and the well known role of trial and appellate judges in limiting excessive jury verdicts "where no reasonable relationship exists between the amount awarded and the injury sustained."[150] Justice White correctly observes that while the majority musters absolutely no empirical evidence to justify its fears, the available information tends to confirm "that American courts have ably discharged this responsibility."[151] As Professor Willard H. Pedrick's widely cited article on freedom of the press and the law of libel concludes, apart from a few "modern sensations" the "American courts have supervised libel awards rather closely."[152] Further, in his early empirical study of the practical utility of jury trials in Michigan, Edson R. Sunderland found that there was very little difference between the decisions of juries and judges in comparable cases.[153] The assumption that juries will rule most often in favor of plaintiffs as against respondents and in favor of individuals as against corporations, and will assess consistently larger amounts as awards, are not borne out by the evidence.[154]

In this case, then, the Court made it more difficult for private individuals to win awards in libel cases, and it did so without a proper basis for this result. In other words, the Court reduced the ability of private individuals to defend their reputations and presented no convincing argument as to why such a reduction is necessary or even desirable.

VI. Why Should We Care?

We now ask: why should we be so concerned about the Court's errors concerning facts, evidence or applicable law? Why should we care? But before we do, it is appropriate to confront the argument of the legal realists. Jerome Frank said more than thirty years ago that "judges make facts." All complicated case records are ambiguous, he argued, and one person's view of the facts will inevitably differ from another's. What is decisive is the background and commitments of the judge.[155] It is certainly true that the records in some cases are ambiguous, that the factual, evidentiary or legal background of some cases is subject to various interpretations. When my research assistants and I found such cases, I decided not to include discussion of them in this essay. As to the cases which are included, it seems clear that the Court did commit serious errors in dealing with the known facts, evidence or law in each case. That is, the facts, evidence or law relevant in each case are so unambiguous that they are not subject to different interpretations based on the background or commitments of the Justices. Of this, of course, the reader must be the final judge. Finally, it should be noted that the argument of the legal realists, when taken to its logical conclusion, involves an internal contradiction: the realists assert as fact that there are no facts, only the perspectives of individuals.[156]

The basic reason for our concern about the factual, evidentiary
and legal errors of the Court must be the effect of the errors on the
decisions in these and other cases. The Court's decisions in *Roe*
and *Mapp* were clearly influenced by the errors committed in
these cases, though the decisions in these cases also rested on
grounds or arguments not affected by the errors; in other words,
the errors committed by the Court contributed to the decisions in
these cases, but that contribution was not dispositive. The
decision in *Roe,* for example, was substantially influenced by the
Court's understanding of a woman's constitutional right to privacy
as well as by the errors discussed earlier. The decision in *Mapp*
was substantially influenced by the Court's understanding of the
exclusionary rule as a protection of individual privacy as well as
by its belief, discussed earlier, that the rule was a deterrent to
improper police searches and seizures.

But in *Swann, Keyes, Arlington Heights, Reynolds, Weber,
Calbeck,* and *Gertz,* the error committed by the Court led directly
to an improper or incorrect result; in these cases, the error was
dispositive in the sense that it forms a necessary part of the Court's
thinking in reaching the result, and the Court's holding would
necessarily have been different had the error not been committed.
For example, the Court could not have ordered busing in *Swann*
had it acknowledged that the relevant schools were not segregated
by law; the Court could not have approved the Kaiser Aluminum
affirmative action plan had it understood the Civil Rights Act of
1964 properly. Generally, then, our concern about all of these
errors is that they may contribute to or lead directly to incorrect
or improper decisions by the Court. The commission of these errors
substantially reduces the Court's ability to engage in proper
policy-making for the nation.

We have not argued here that the various errors discussed were
committed intentionally. We have not argued that the Justices
manipulate the facts to fit a desired outcome and fashion the
outcome to fit their private notions of what is desirable public
policy. In short, we have not made out a case that these errors are
attributable to result-orientation on the part of the Justices. However, to whatever extent these errors were committed intentionally,

to that extent the Justices are not living up to the almost universal expectation that judges, but especially Supreme Court Justices, attempt to the greatest possible degree to be fair, impartial and unbiased.

Such impartiality was clearly the expectation of the founding fathers, as expressed in that pre-eminent commentary on the Constitution, *The Federalist:*

> It can be of no weight to say that the courts, on the pretence of a repugnancy, may substitute their own pleasure to the constitutional intentions of the legislature. This might as well happen in the case of two contradictory statutes; or it might as well happen in every adjudication upon any single statute. The courts must declare the sense of the law; and if they should be disposed to exercise WILL instead of JUDGMENT, the consequence would equally be the substitution of their pleasure to that of the legislative body. The observation, if it prove anything, would prove that there ought to be no judges distinct from that body.

> If, then, the courts of justice are to be considered as the bulwarks of a limited Constitution against legislative encroachments, this consideration will afford a strong argument for the permanent tenure of judicial offices since nothing will contribute so much as this to that independent spirit in the judges which must be essential to the faithful performance of so arduous a duty.[157]

Clearly, Justice Frankfurter thought that the Court majority had engaged in result-oriented jurisprudence when he said in his dissent in *Baker v. Carr,* "Unless judges, the judges of this Court, are to make their private views of political wisdom the measure of the Constitution . . . the Fourteenth Amendment provides no guide for judicial oversight of the representation problem."[158] And Justice Harlan had similar thoughts when he said in dissent in *Mapp:* "I do not believe that the Fourteenth Amendment empowers this Court to mold state remedies effectuating the right to freedom from 'arbitrary intrusion by the police' to suit its own notions of how things should be done. . . ."[159]

VII. Looking to the Future

What could be done, what steps could be taken, to prevent or deal with the sorts of errors discussed in this study? First, we must point out and criticize the errors of the Court more often and more effectively than heretofore; we must, in other words, carry on the important work of this kind undertaken by Alexander Bickel and Henry Abraham,[160] among others. We must, as these scholars have done, insist on the very highest standards of scholarship and craftsmanship in High Court decisions, qualities which are so conspicuously lacking in the decisions discussed here. The purpose of this sort of review of the work of the Supreme Court is to make the Justices increasingly aware of the kinds of errors discussed here, and the possibility of their making such errors, and to encourage the Justices, where appropriate, to modify or reverse their previous decisions in light of these errors.

The activities described above take place to a large extent in the nation's law reviews. This being true, one must ask: do the Supreme Court Justices pay attention to law review articles? If not, no amount of criticism, however well documented, reasoned and argued, could sway their opinions. Both a review of scholarly opinion on the topic and an examination of some opinions of the Supreme Court support the idea that law review criticism has, at least, a chance of hitting the mark.

The consensus of scholarly opinion regarding the influence of law review articles on Supreme Court decision-making seems clear. Professor Henry Abraham says in *The Judicial Process:* "jurists are part of the legal process and are quite naturally generally familiar with the thinking that presents itself in the pages of [law] reviews. . . ."[161] But mere awareness of what is discussed is insufficient to show the influence wielded by the law reviews. Professor Peltason argues that:

> Law reviews published by law schools, the journals published by bar associations, and professional books do for judicial decisions what the drama critics' reviews do for a Broadway play. "It was the law journals reversing the decisions of the Supreme Court, which led the fight on the Old Court," . . . [I]t may be that the Supreme Court follows not the election returns but the law reviews.[162]

Professor Glendon Schubert supports Peltason's analysis of the influence of scholarly criticism on the Supreme Court. In *Judicial Policy-Making,* he states his views, bringing to bear examples of the reliance by the Court on law reviews:

> Members of the Supreme Court rely upon the law reviews to provide them with supporting arguments and rationales which they then can and do cite in their opinions in support of their decisions. The rationale for the Court's recent major decision . . . in *Baker v. Carr* was taken directly from the brief submitted by Solicitor General Cox, which in turn relied heavily upon a then recent article in the *Harvard Law Review* written by the newspaperman who covered the Supreme Court for the *New York Times.*[163]

It does seem that those who write in law reviews may have access to the Court. In fact, as Abraham claims:

> There is no doubt that reliance on the legal periodicals by both bar and courts during the past generation or so has increased. Although difficult to determine objectively, this particular genre of the written word exerts a formative influence. . . .[164]

Only one systematic study has been undertaken to attempt to document the contentions of law review influence. Chester A. Newland examined the Supreme Court from its October 1924 term through the October term, 1956, and found a measurable increase in law review citations within the final twenty-year period of his study.[165] He noted that, although during the New Deal only the Roosevelt appointees cited legal periodicals with regularity, the practice soon became generalized. The "ivy league" reviews, primarily that of Harvard, were most often relied upon.[166] Newland provides examples of several uses of law reviews. In *Erie Railroad v. Tompkins*,[167] Justice Brandeis' opinion, relying on a *Harvard Law Review* article by Charles Warren,[168] overruled the earlier decision in *Swift v. Tyson*.[169] Justice Brandeis cited twenty-one other articles in the same opinion. Justice Frankfurter, in *O'Malley v. Woodrough*,[170] cited articles from the *Yale Law Journal*, the *Iowa Law Review*,[171] and several case notes from various legal periodicals.[172] Newland's work, basically quantitative, points to the problem of attributing influence to arguments from reviews on the basis of mere citation. He points out, for example, that in *Senior v. Braden*[173] the articles cited appeared to have only a small influence on the opinion, and Justice McReynolds rejected flatly the only article he cited within the period of the study.[174]

An extension of the period of Newland's study (although admittedly less thorough) to encompass fifty Supreme Court decisions between the years 1903 and 1976, generally supports his initial findings (see Table 1). Of the cases examined, the lowest number of citations was found before 1931, with the highest number found in 1972. In the sixteen cases falling prior to 1941, only six legal periodicals were cited, while the next eighteen cases (falling between 1941 and 1965) contained forty-five citations; the final sixteen cases cited one hundred fifteen law review articles.

None of the studies of the influence of legal periodicals on Supreme Court decision-making have demonstrated without doubt that such articles have a decisive impact on the way the Justices decide their cases. To do so would require extensive research not only on the cases themselves, but on the articles cited as well. But the opinion of legal scholars, and the available evidence that judges are increasingly using law reviews, whether to gather support for their opinions or to form those opinions, make it possible to consider legal periodicals to be a potentially

Table 1

Cases Examined	Citation and Date of Decision	Number of Law Review Articles Cited
The Lottery Case	188 U.S. 321 (1903)	0
Lochner v. New York	198 U.S. 45 (1905)	0
Muskrat v. United States	219 U.S. 346 (1911)	0
Houston East and West Ry. v. United States (The Shreveport Case)	234 U.S. 342 (1914)	0
Hammer v. Dagenhart	247 U.S. 251 (1918)	0
Schenck v. United States	249 U.S. 47 (1919)	0
Bailey v. Drexel Furniture	259 U.S. 20 (1922)	0
Gitlow v. New York	268 U.S. 652 (1925)	0
Olmstead v. United States	277 U.S. 438 (1928)	0
Near v. Minnesota	283 U.S. 697 (1931)	2
United States v. Butler	297 U.S. 1 (1935)	0
United States v. Curtiss-Wright Export	299 U.S. 304 (1936)	0
Carter v. Carter Coal Co.	298 U.S. 238 (1936)	0
NLRB v. Jones & Laughlin Steel	301 U.S. 1 (1936)	0
Palko v. Connecticut	302 U.S. 319 (1937)	2
Coleman v. Miller	307 U.S. 433 (1939)	2
Hines v. Davidowitz	312 U.S. 52 (1941)	0
United States v. Darby	312 U.S. 100 (1941)	0
Smith v. Allwright	321 U.S. 649 (1944)	0
Adamson v. California	332 U.S. 46 (1947)	10
Wolf v. Colorado	338 U.S. 25 (1949)	2
Dennis v. United States	341 U.S. 494 (1951)	2
Youngstown Sheet & Tube v. Sawyer	343 U.S. 579 (1952)	1
Brown v. Board of Education of Topeka	347 U.S. 483 (1954)	0 (however, many social science journals were cited)

Cases Examined (contd.)	Citations and Date of Decision (contd.)	Number of Law Review Articles Cited (contd.)
Yates v. United States	354 U.S. 298 (1957)	1
Barenblatt v. United States	360 U.S. 109 (1959)	3
Braunfeld v. Brown	366 U.S. 599 (1961)	0
Mapp v. Ohio	367 U.S. 643 (1961)	0
Manual Enterprises, Inc. v. Day	370 U.S. 478 (1962)	3
Baker v. Carr	369 U.S. 186 (1962)	12
Gideon v. Wainwright	372 U.S. 335 (1963)	3
Heart of Atlanta Motel v. United States	379 U.S. 241 (1964)	0
Katzenbach v. McClung	379 U.S. 294 (1964)	0
Reynolds v. Sims	377 U.S. 533 (1964)	8
Griswold v. Connecticut	381 U.S. 479 (1965)	8
Miranda v. Arizona	384 U.S. 436 (1966)	36
Flast v. Cohen	392 U.S. 83 (1968)	12
Shapiro v. Thompson	394 U.S. 618 (1969)	1
Brandenburg v. Ohio	395 U.S. 444 (1969)	1
New York Times v. United States	403 U.S. 713 (1971)	0
Apodaca v. Oregon	406 U.S. 404 (1972)	7
Gravel v. United States	408 U.S. 606 (1972)	7
Furman v. Georgia	408 U.S. 238 (1972)	45
Roe v. Wade	410 U.S. 113 (1973)	12
Frontiero v. Richardson	411 U.S. 677 (1973)	5
Paris Adult Theatre I v. Slaton	413 U.S. 49 (1973)	5
Miller v. California	413 U.S. 15 (1973)	0
United States v. Nixon	418 U.S. 683 (1974)	0
Murphy v. Florida	421 U.S. 794 (1975)	0
Stone v. Powell	428 U.S. 465 (1976)	15

constructive influence on the Court. It is undoubtedly true that the law reviews are only as good as the individuals who write in them—their quality obviously varies—and that the influence of law reviews has not uniformly been salutary.[175] Yet the fact that the Justices, or at least their law clerks, read the reviews and cite them, opens an important avenue for the critical analysis of decisions by competent persons, and for the possibility that the law reviews could increasingly be watchdogs against the kinds of serious errors discussed earlier.

Second, there must be an increased level of informed public awareness and discussion of Supreme Court decisions, led by print and electronic media, political leaders and especially by commentators. Such awareness and discussion may influence the Court's deliberations and, at the very least, will influence those responsible for choosing the members of the Court. As one increases the level of the public's awareness of the work of the High Court, it becomes more likely that the Court's errors will be widely known and criticized. Such errors become increasingly costly and embarrassing for the Court. We are not suggesting here that the Court become in any sense trendy or that it simply follow or be guided by the election returns. We are merely stating a fairly obvious point: that public exposure of the Court's errors can have a salutary impact on the Court.

The need for a greater degree of public awareness of the Court's work is made clear by a study of the public image of courts undertaken for the National Center for State Courts by Yankelovich, Skelly, and White, Inc.[176] That study concluded that the general public's knowledge of American courts is low. For example, 72% of the public incorrectly believes that the United States Supreme Court can review and reverse any decision made by a state court.[177] Further, the study concludes that there is a widespread public opinion that media should play an expanded role in showing how the federal and state courts work, how effectively they operate, and what they do.[178]

What could be done to remedy the public's lack of knowledge about the courts, especially about the Supreme Court and its decisions?

As a beginning, newspapers should attempt to do a more comprehensive job of reporting Supreme Court activities. As was indicated by one recent study of *New York Times* coverage of Supreme Court decisions, "Relying strictly on the *Times,* a reader still would not know what really happened in more than three-fourths of the Court's decisions of the 1974 October term— not to mention why it happened and with what consequences for the reader."[179] That same study concludes that "not only do Supreme Court decisions compete against other news of the day for space . . . but they compete against each other for space."[180] We should of course bear in mind that *New York Times* coverage of the decisions of the United States Supreme Court is more comprehensive than that of almost all other newspapers. But of course quantity of discussion is not enough. As we have recently witnessed with the *Bakke* and *Weber* decisions, there is often much comment after a major Supreme Court decision comes down as to whose ox did or did not get gored. Rather, what is needed is a recognition on the part of the media, civic leaders and political commentators that the Court's role is one of constitutional and statutory interpretation, not distribution of resources. Thus, commentary on High Court decisions should focus on the quality of the Court's work and, therefore, should insist that the Court adhere to high standards of accuracy, rigor and logic in applying the Constitution and the laws to the concrete issues before it.

Chief Justice Burger has initiated the helpful practice of providing the press not only with copies of the full decision but with synopses tailored to fit their needs. To assist the media in improving their coverage of the Court's rulings, "PREVIEW of United States Supreme Court Cases" was developed several years ago. It is a public service produced by the American Law Institute—American Bar Association Committee on Continuing Professional Education and the Association of American Law Schools. Each memorandum is prepared by an experienced law school professor in concise, one-page analyses so as to facilitate rapid identification of the issues that were critical in the case and of the probable impact of the Court's holding. PREVIEW has received the support of Chief Justice Burger, who has stated that "PREVIEW has improved the news coverage of the decisions of the Court."[181] Former Chief Justice Warren also supported the project.

Second, by far the most controversial suggestion to improve public knowledge and awareness of the Court is that of allowing the media to televise oral arguments, decision announcements, or both.[182] The Supreme Court has refused to allow such access to its public proceedings. But it is unclear why such a potentially profitable undertaking should not be seriously considered. The argument that judges (and Justices) will "grandstand" or play to the cameras appears to be unsubstantiated. The experiment with televised trials in Florida and Georgia has proven to be at least moderately successful, with no evidence of the "circus atmosphere" deplored in the sensational Lindbergh kidnapping case and others in the early days of broadcast journalism.[183] The provision that video-tapes of Supreme Court proceedings be exempt from newsroom editing, perhaps shown only in their entirety on public broadcast networks, should calm those who fear that the electronic media could edit tapes to create misimpressions of Court decisions.

In short, the Supreme Court itself needs to consider carefully what role it should play in informing the public more fully about its work—a public anxious to be educated.

Third, the Court should consider seriously a judicial overturning or modification of those decisions, including the ones discussed earlier, which are premised either wholly or substantially on error. The Court is of course on solid ground when it approaches with great caution the problem of modifying or reversing its previous decisions, for continuity of precedent is clearly desirable. Public respect for the law and for the Court and compliance with the Court's orders cannot be enhanced by all-too-frequent changes in that law. On the other hand, the public interest is badly served by failure to retreat from error; and for those more or less knowledgeable about the work of the Court, such failure does little to improve the Court's reputation. In deciding which decisions to modify or reverse, the Court would need to weigh in the balance these considerations.

One additional point should be made here: the possibility that a decision will be overruled or modified should incline those Justices who support that decision, and especially the Justice who writes that decision, to be vigilant against committing errors.

Fourth, both the Justice Department and the American Bar Association's Standing Committee on the Federal Judiciary should be strongly encouraged, when they are conducting investigations of the background and qualifications of potential Supreme Court Justices, to search for and to identify individuals whose previous judicial decisions or other writings or speeches are characterized by the sorts of errors discussed here. This may require closer scrutiny of the writing of candidates or nominees than has previously been the case; it may also require consultation with experts in relevant fields.

Fifth, as to those cases like *Calbeck* and *Weber* which involve statutory interpretation, Congress should be encouraged to "overrule" the Court's decision by amending the relevant legislation in such a way as to preclude expressly the Court's interpretation. In this way, Congress leaves no doubt about the nature of its intentions. From time to time, Congress has chosen this means to negate Supreme Court decisions, for example in its reaction to *Tennessee Valley Authority v. Hill*,[184] the recent case involving the snail darter. More frequent use of this device when the Supreme Court misunderstands or misinterprets the will of Congress would serve as a reminder to the Court to be extremely careful in its construction of statutes. Congress may wish to establish a committee to advise it on desirable changes in federal legislation—changes aimed at preserving congressional intent when, in the view of that committee, the federal courts have not given effect to that intent.

If congressional sentiment is sufficiently strong and if the constitutional issue is of the greatest importance, Congress has the power to propose amendments to the Constitution which modify or reverse Supreme Court decisions. There are currently before Congress a number of proposed constitutional amendments whose effect would be to modify or reverse Supreme Court decisions affecting such matters as abortion[185] and school busing.[186] In the past, Congress has reacted nine times to a Supreme Court decision interpreting the Constitution by recommending that the document be amended; such recommendations played a key role in the adoption of the Eleventh, Thirteenth, Fourteenth, Fifteenth, Sixteenth, and Twenty-Sixth Amendments. This is not a procedure to be undertaken lightly, but in the constitutional amendment process, the long-term stability of the law is protected by the necessity to secure ratification of a proposed amendment by three-fourths of the state legislatures; this requirement also reduces the likelihood of the adoption of improvident amendments.

Sixth, it seems inappropriate that the principle of *stare decisis* should apply to those elements of a case which are of a factual or evidentiary nature; this is true because factual conclusions drawn by the Court can be shown to be fundamentally wrong or to be outdated in the light of new evidence. Federal district court judges ought to have the authority to "challenge" Supreme Court factual conclusions, either because they were wrong from the start or because they are wrong in the light of new evidence. If the circuit court agrees with the district court, then it is apparent that the Supreme Court should review carefully its earlier conclusions. Such a procedure would give the Supreme Court Justices a greater incentive to be careful in their initial fact-finding. Such challenges would take place infrequently and, therefore, the caseload of the appellate courts and the Supreme Court would increase only slightly. The greatest benefit of such challenges, however, would be the continual scrutiny they would provide for the factual and evidentiary conclusions of the Supreme Court.

Seventh, a number of scholars, as well as a substantial number of Supreme Court Justices, have written extensively about the Court being burdened with too great a workload.[187] Indeed, a number of plans have been developed for reducing that workload.[188] It is certainly worth inquiring whether the Court's errors may, at least partially, be attributed to the need to complete its large volume of business and, if this is the case, whether it is not time to take action to reduce that volume of business. If the Court is committing serious errors in its cases because it lacks the time to research and consider its opinions adequately, we must weigh seriously the sort of reduction in workload for the Court which will allow that body to give its cases the attention they obviously deserve. On the subject of the impact of the Court's workload on the quality of its opinions, one should note carefully the words of Professor Henry M. Hart, Jr., written twenty-two years ago when the Court's workload was much smaller than it is currently:

> If what has just been said is accepted, the conclusion emerges inexorably that the number of cases which the Supreme Court tries to decide by full opinion, far from being increased, ought to be materially decreased. An average of twenty-four hours may be enough time, or more than enough, in which to prepare a superficially plausible rationalization of what is in substance an *ipse dixit.* It may even be enough time in which to prepare a genuinely workmanlike opinion which accurately reports the facts or record and the issues arising out of them and deals systematically and conscientiously with all the contentions of counsel and the relevant precedents which counsel cite. But opinions which bring to problems the fresh illumination of personal research and of hard, independent thought cannot be written that fast. . . .
>
> The opinions of the Justices, if one turns to them, confirm the conclusion that the Court is trying to decide more cases than it can decide well. Regretfully and with deference, it has to be said that too many of the Court's opinions are about what one would expect could be written in twenty-four hours. There are able opinions, to be sure, including many that have manifestly taken much more time than that in thought and composition. But few of the Court's opinions, far too few, genuinely illumine the area of law with which they deal. Other opinions fail even by much more elementary standards. Issues are ducked which in good lawyership and good conscience ought not to be ducked. Technical mistakes are made which ought not to be made in decisions of the Supreme Court of the United States.[189]

Finally, a number of suggestions have been made to improve the Supreme Court's fact-finding process, suggestions which would, if adopted, decrease the likelihood of the Court's making the sorts of errors described here. Professors Miller and Barron have suggested that when facts are central to the Court's decision-making and when these facts are complex or doubtful, the Court should consider remanding for factual development.[190] For example, a remand may well have been helpful in *Gertz* in an attempt to determine the validity of the claims of the press, or in *Mapp* in an attempt to determine the probable deterrent impact of an exclusionary rule. Such remands would be consistent with the "orthodox model of the appellate process."[191] On the other hand, as Miller and Barron point out, "It is doubtful whether the Supreme Court will be eager to have questions of legislative fact in matters of vital social policy decided by federal district judges."[192] Professor Davis adds that a remand to an agency might be preferable to a remand to a court

> . . . because the trial court's procedure is likely to be the same as it would be for finding adjudicative facts. Use of the Federal Rules of Evidence, along with full freedom to cross-examine, may be wholly inappropriate. . . . Most trial judges are similarly likely to follow their usual habits about both cross-examination and exclusion of hearsay, even though the habits about both are usually ill-suited to developing legislative facts.[193]

When facts are central to decision-making in the Supreme Court, Professor Davis has further suggested that the Court ask the parties to provide factual briefs and that, in appropriate cases, the Court provide an opportunity for each party to challenge the facts provided by the other party.[194] Such procedures would have several advantages: they would provide the litigants with an added measure of procedural fairness in that they would provide a pre-decision opportunity to challenge the facts upon which the Court may rely. And they would in many cases give the Court a wider and deeper appreciation of the facts than it presently enjoys. Certainly, the Court would have been aided by such factual briefs in addressing the problem of deterrence in *Mapp* or in evaluating the claims of the press in *Gertz* or in understanding the status in law of unborn children in *Roe*.

A further suggestion for improving the Court's fact-finding process is made by Professors Miller and Barron. It frequently happens that the relevance of certain facts becomes clear only as the Court is deliberating about its decision in a particular case. Miller and Barron suggest:

> . . . the Court could ask counsel for further briefs on a particular point. The Court does so on occasion now. The Court should strive to determine the views of counsel where a case appears to involve an assessment of data never considered by the trial court or which does not appear plainly in the briefs submitted to the Supreme Court.[195]

Finally, I suggest that the Supreme Court, and indeed all federal courts, should operate under a rule which obligates them to explain clearly the source and the basis of each of their factual conclusions. This sort of a rule would proscribe the kinds of unsupported factual assertions made by the majority in *Gertz,* in *Mapp* and in *Roe.* Justices and judges ought not to be allowed to employ facts in their decisions which have little or no validity except in the mind of the judge. An assertion does not become a fact simply because a judge believes it.

Generally, improvement in the Supreme Court's decision-making process would be highly desirable. As Miller and Barron point out:

> It is incumbent on the Justices not to resort to blind guesses about the effect of their decisions or to an uncritical acceptance of data. The Justices should do their best to inform themselves about all relevant data concerning a given issue of great public interest.[196]

VIII. Conclusion

We have attempted to show that the Justices of the United States Supreme Court, in dealing with the facts, evidence, and applicable law in a variety of cases, have committed four types of errors; we have provided a number of examples of each type of error. We have discussed the importance of these errors in the judicial process. Finally, we have put forward a number of suggestions for preventing or reducing the occurrence of these errors.

Justice Robert Jackson put his finger on the importance of our subject when he said:

> The purpose of a hearing is that the Court may learn what it does not know, and it knows least about the facts. It may sound paradoxical, but most contentions of law are won or lost on the facts. They often incline a judge to one side or the other.[197]

Notes

1. Berle, The Three Faces of Power 1 (1967): "Ultimate legislative power in the United States has come to rest in the Supreme Court of the United States." Funston, Constitutional Counterrevolution 4–7 (1977); Kurland, Toward a Political Supreme Court, 37 U. Chi. L. Rev. 19 (1969); Goodwin, The Shape of American Politics, 43 Commentary 25, 26–27 (June 1967): "The nine justices of the Supreme Court make major political decisions, unresponsive to the democratic process in secret meetings on Friday afternoons. Both the number and the scope of such decisions steadily mount. Liberal critics have generally approved this development, because they approve the content of decisions, while the fundamental reshaping of an important institution seems not to trouble them. But it is a transformation which almost certainly will come back to plague us as judicial personnel and social attitudes change, and as an institution which has become more and more political develops an ever greater sensitivity to transitory shifts in political temper."

2. Shapiro, The Supreme Court from Warren to Burger, in King, ed., The New American Political System 179 (1978).

3. *See,* for example, Sowle, Knowledge and Decision (1981).

4. *See* Cummings and Wise, Democracy under Pressure: An Introduction to the American Political System 456–58 (1981).

5. 377 U.S. 533 (1964).

6. *Id.* at 564–65.

7. 367 U.S. 643 (1961).

8. *Id.* at 656.

9. 443 U.S. 193 (1979).

10. *Id.* at 200–08.

11. 429 U.S. 252 (1977).

12. *Id.* at 268–71.

13. 418 U.S. 323 (1974).

14. *Id.* at 349.

15. Bickel, The Supreme Court and the Idea of Progress 47–100 (1978); *see also* Corwin, The Steel Seizure Case: A Judicial Brick Without Straw, 53 Col. L. Rev. 53 (1953).

16. Hart, The Supreme Court, 1963 Term-Forward: The Time Chart of the Judges, 73 Harv. L. Rev. 85, 99–100 (1964).

17. Funston, *supra* note 1, at 297–367 (1977).

18. Abraham, Some Post-Bakke-and-Weber Reflections on Reverse Discrimination, 14 U. Rich. L. Rev. 373 (1980).

19. 402 U.S. 1 (1971).

20. 347 U.S. 483 (1954) and 349 U.S. 294 (1955)—commonly referred to as "Brown I" and "Brown II," respectively.

21. 402 U.S. at 15.

22. *Id.* at 30.

23. *Id.* at 15.

24. Graglia, The Supreme Court: Abuse of Power, 30 National Review 892, 895 (July 21, 1978). For a similar statement as well as relevant documentation, *see* Graglia, Disaster by Decree, 108–09 citing Record 323a, 744a–46a; and 125–26 (1976).

25. Part of the Court's justification in *Swann* for its approval of the district judge's "very limited use of mathematical ratios" to determine the racial composition of Charlotte-Mecklenburg's schools was as follows:

> The predicate for the District Court's use of the 71%–29% ratio was twofold: first, its express finding, approved by the Court of Appeals and not challenged here, that a dual school system had been maintained by the school authorities at least until 1969; second, its finding, also approved by the Court of Appeals, that the school board had totally defaulted in its acknowledged duty to come forward with an acceptable plan of its own, notwithstanding the patient efforts of the District Judge who, on at least three occasions, urged the board to submit plans. 402 U.S. at 24.

But Professor Graglia has shown that this statement is inaccurate in almost every respect:

First, the board had not maintained an unconstitutional dual system until 1969; the district court in 1965 and the Fourth Circuit, en banc, in 1966 held that the board had achieved a constitutional system by 1965 at least. In the present round of litigation, the district court explicitly found that the board had complied in good faith with those earlier decisions. The Court's implication that new requirements were justified by a failure to comply with prior ones was, therefore, baseless.

Second, the board had not "totally defaulted" in its duty to come forward with an acceptable plan, unless its offering a plan that would have eliminated all majority-black senior high schools and all such junior high schools except one that had not been a black school under the dual system can be described as a total default. The constitutional deficiency of at least these parts of the board's plan is not apparent even with the aid of the Court's decision that they were properly rejected. Finally, it does not appear that the district court found that the board had "totally defaulted" in presenting its plan, and in any event, the court of appeals clearly had not "approved" any such finding. On the contrary, the two court of appeals judges who would have affirmed the district court's decision in all respects complained that "the majority implies that the actions of this Board have been exemplary." 431 F.2d 154, n. 9. Even when he did refer to the case before him, Chief Justice Burger seemed to be referring to some other case. Graglia, Disaster by Decree, *supra* note 24 at 123.

26. 413 U.S. 189 (1973).
27. 313 F. Supp. 61 (1970).
28. 413 U.S. at 192.
29. 313 F. Supp. at 73. While holding that the actions of the School Board in areas of the district other than Park Hill were insufficient to dictate the conclusion that this was *de jure* segregation which called for an all-out effort to desegregate, the district court went on to find that the segregated core city schools were educationally inferior to the predominantly white Anglo schools in other parts of the district. Since the School Board must at a constitutional minimum offer equal educational opportunity, the court formulated a remedial plan which provided compensatory education in an integrated environment.
30. 413 U.S. at 201–03.

31. *See generally,* 303 F. Supp. 279, 282 (1969); 313 F. Supp. 61, 69 (1970).

32. *See* Graglia, Disaster by Decree, *supra* note 24, at 182.

33. 313 F. Supp. at 69. "The evidentiary as well as legal approach to the remaining schools is quite different from that which has been outlined above. For one thing, the concentration of minorities occurred at an earlier date, and, in some instances, prior to the *Brown* decision by the Supreme Court. Community attitudes were different, including the attitudes of the School Board members. Furthermore, the transitions were much more gradual and less perceptible than they were in the Park Hill schools."

34. 429 U.S. 252 (1977).

35. 426 U.S. 229 (1976).

36. 429 U.S. at 269.

37. *Id.*

38. Schwemm, From *Washington* to *Arlington Heights* and Beyond: Discriminatory Purpose in Equal Protection Litigation, 1977 U. Ill. L. F. 961, 1027 (1977).

39. "*See* Plaintiffs' Exhibits 48–1, 48–2, 48–3, 48–7, 48–9 (copy on file at the office of the University of Illinois Law Forum). One letter from a local resident appearing in the *Arlington Heights Herald* a month before the first Plan Commission hearing began:

> Concerning your editorial, "Housing: An Ignored Issue": it isn't ignored, it's unwanted. We do resist low-income housing because it is a ploy to export blacks from Chicago to integrate the suburbs. That came out forcefully in the St. Viator Housing proposal.

Another letter complained:

> I'm a bit tired of hearing and reading about the Low Income Housing in Arlington Heights for the benefit of our colored and Spanish-American friends in Chicago. One wonders who is running our village, our [Village President] Walsh or Mayor Daley.

Respondents' Brief, *supra* note 362, at 17–18." [author's footnote]

40. Schwemm, *supra* note 38, at 1027.

41. *Id.* at 1028.

42. Lower courts considering claims similar to the plaintiffs' in *Arlington Heights* have recognized the probative value of evidence of white hostility in establishing that official action excluding subsidized housing was racially motivated. *See, e.g., Park View Heights Corp. v. City of Black Jack,* 467 F.2d 1208, 1210 (8th Cir. 1972); *Kennedy Park Homes Ass'n v. City of Lackawanna,* 436 F.2d 108, 113 (2d Cir. 1970), *cert. denied,* 301 U.S. 1010 (1971); *Dailey v. City of Lawton,*

425 F.2d 1037, 1039 (10th Cir. 1970); *Resident Advisory Bd. v. Rizzo,* 425 F. Supp. 987 (E.D. Pa. 1976), *aff'd,* 564 F.2d 126 (3d Cir. 1977). [author's footnote].

43. Brief for Respondents at 19, *Village of Arlington Heights v. Metropolitan Hous. Dev. Corp.,* 429 U.S. 252 (1977) (copy on file at the office of University of Illinois Law Forum). [author's footnote] This statement was made in the official minutes of the meeting of the Arlington Heights Board of Trustees at which the housing proposal was rejected.

44. Professor Schwemm calls attention to another problem with the Court's use and evaluation of evidence in this case:

> *Arlington Heights* continued the Supreme Court's tradition of extreme deference to municipal zoning decisions. Justice Powell's opinion accepted both the village's concern for neighboring property values and its claim that the MHDC proposal was inconsistent with its buffer policy. He concluded that "[t]here is no reason to doubt" that some local homeowners had relied on the maintenance of single-family zoning in the area. 429 U.S. at 270. Actually, this claim was subject to considerable doubt. First, the builders of the neighboring houses could not have relied on the comprehensive zoning plan, because their houses were built years before the plan was adopted. *See* Respondent's Brief, *supra* note at 34n. Even if the homes had been sold to new owners after the adoption of the plan, the new residents certainly could not expect all of the Viatorian land to remain vacant indefinitely. They should have known that when it was developed it could be used for apartments, because Arlington Heights had permitted multiple-family developments next to every other high school in the village. *Id.* at 11n. In fact, the Court should not have treated the reliance claim as a separate defense at all. The claim is meaningless apart from a consideration of the zoning aspects of the MHDC proposal, because only *reasonable* reliance deserves judicial protection and what is reasonable depends on how the village's legitimate zoning policies applied to the MHDC site. Local homeowners, for example, could not have a reasonable reliance interest in enforcing a zoning scheme against MHDC that specifically provided that only whites live on the Viatorian property. *Metropolitan Hous. Dev. Corp. v. Village of Arlington Heights,* 517 F.2d 409, 415 (7th Cir. 1975).

Schwemm, *supra* note 38, at 1032.

45. Letter from Professor Schwemm to the author, September 7, 1982. Professor Schwemm is Professor of Law at the University of Kentucky College of Law.

46. 429 U.S. at 265–66 and n. 21.

47. 377 U.S. 533 (1964).

48. *Lucas v. Forty-Fourth General Assembly,* 377 U.S. 713 (1964) (Colorado); *WMCA, Inc. v. Lomenzo,* 377 U.S. 633 (1964) (New York); *Maryland Committee for Fair Representation v. Tawes,* 377 U.S. 656 (1964) (Maryland); *Davis v. Mann,* 377 U.S. 678 (1964) (Virginia); *Roman v. Sincock,* 377 U.S. 695 (1964) (Delaware).

49. 377 U.S. at 565–66, 568.

50. *Supra* note 48.

51. 377 U.S. at 565–66.

52. 369 U.S. 186 (1962).

53. *Id.* at 301 (Frankfurter, J., dissenting).

54. 377 U.S. at 574–75.

55. *Id.*

56. Calhoun said: "Ours is not a Government of precedents, nor can they be admitted, except to a very limited extent, and with great caution in the interpretation of the Constitution, without changing in time, the entire character of the instrument. The only safe rule is the Constitution itself,—or, if that be doubtful, the history of the times." South Carolina Exposition and Protest, reprinted in Frisch & Stevens, The Political Thought of American Statesmen 122 (1973).

57. *Avery v. Midland County,* 390 U.S. 474 (1968); *Hadley v. Junior College District,* 397 U.S. 50, 56 (1970):

> ... as a general rule, whenever a state or local government decides to select persons by popular election to perform governmental functions, the Equal Protection Clause of the Fourteenth Amendment requires that each qualified voter must be given an equal opportunity to participate in that election, and when members of an elected body are chosen from separate districts, each district must be established on a basis which will insure as far as practicable, that equal numbers of voters can vote for proportionally equal numbers of officials.

58. *See* O'Rourke, Reapportionment: Law, Politics, Computers (1972).

59. 377 U.S. at 755–56 (Stewart J., dissenting) (1964).

60. 410 U.S. 113 (1973).

61. 410 U.S. 179 (1973).

62. *Roe,* 410 U.S. at 163–64.

63. *Id.* at 160 citing Hellman & Pritchard, Williams Obstetrics 493 (14th ed. 1971); Dorland's Illustrated Medical Dictionary 1980 (24th ed. 1965).

64. *Id.*

65. Byrn, An American Tragedy: The Supreme Court on Abortion, 41 Ford. L. Rev. 807 (1973).

66. *Id.* at 815–27.

67. *Id.* at 827–35.

68. *Id.* at 835–39.

69. 410 U.S. at 151 (footnote omitted).

70. *State v. Murphy,* 27 N.J.L. 112 (Sup. Ct. 1858).

71. Byrn, *supra* note 65, at 827–28.

72. *See State v. Gedicke,* 43 N.J. L. 86, 90 (Sup. Ct. 1881); *Trent v. State,* 15 Ala. App. 485, 488, 73 So. 834, 836 (1916), *cert. denied* 198 Ala. 695, 73 So. 1002 (1917); *Dougherty v. People,* 1 Colo. 514, 522 (1872). *State v. Moore,* 25 Iowa 128, 135–36 (1868); *People v. Sessions,* 58 Mich. 594, 596, 26 N.W. 291, 293 (1886).

73. *Dougherty v. People, id.* at 522.

74. *Trent v. State, id.* at 488.

75. 410 U.S. at 161.

76. *Id.* at 162.

77. Note, The Law and the Unborn Child: The Legal and Logical Inconsistencies, 46 Notre Dame Lawyer 349 (1971).

78. *Id.* at 351–54.

79. *Id.* at 358.

80. *Id.* at 360.

81. 370 U.S. 114 (1962).

82. *Id.* at 131–32.

83. 33 U.S.C. Section 903 (a) (1926) provides:

(a) Compensation shall be payable under this chapter in respect of disability or death of an employee, but only if the disability or death results from an injury occurring upon the navigable waters of the United States (including any dry dock) and if recovery for the disability or death through workmen's compensation proceedings may not validly be provided by State law. No compensation shall be payable in respect of the disability or death of

(1) A master or member of a crew of any vessel, nor any

person engaged by the master to load or unload or repair any
small vessel under eighteen tons net; or
(2) An officer or employee of the United States or foreign
government or of any political subdivision thereof.

84. 370 U.S. at 117–18.
85. *Id.* at 118–19.
86. *Id.* at 120–22.
87. *Id.* at 121–22.
88. *Id.* at 132 (Stewart, J., dissenting).
89. *Id.* at 127.
90. *See generally, id.* at 121–23.
91. Hearings Before the Senate Judiciary Committee on S. 3170,
69th Cong., 1st Sess. 84 (1926). For similar statements made during the
committee hearings on the proposed legislation, see Hearings Before the
House Judiciary Committee on H.R. 9498, 69th Cong., 1st Sess. at 39,
81 (1926); Hearings Before the Oversight Subcommittee on S. 3170,
69th Cong., 1st Sess. at 22, 25–27, 31, 38, 85 (1926).
92. S. Rep. No. 973, 69th Cong., 1st Sess. at 16 (1926).
93. H.R. Rep. No. 1190, 69th Cong., 1st Sess. at 3 (1926).
94. *See* 370 U.S. at 133.
95. 374 U.S. 449 (1963).
96. 8 U.S.C. Section 1101 (a) (1952) provides:

The term entry means any coming of an alien into the United
States, from a foreign port or place or from an outlying possession,
whether voluntarily or otherwise, except that an alien having a
lawful permanent residence in the United States shall not be
regarded as making an entry into the United States for the purposes
of the immigration laws if the alien proves to the satisfaction of the
Attorney General that his departure to a foreign port or place or
to an outlying possession was not intended or reasonably to be
expected by him or his presence in a foreign port or place or outlying possession was not voluntary: Provided, that no person whose
departure from the United States was occasioned by deportation
proceedings, extradition, or other legal process shall be held to
be entitled to such exception.

97. The 1952 Act became effective on December 24, 1952, and
Fleuti entered the country for permanent residence on October 9, 1952,
a fact which is of significance because Section 241 (a) (1) of the Act
commands only the deportation of aliens "excludable by the law existing

at the time of such entry. . . ." Hence, since Fleuti's homosexuality did not make him excludable by any law existing at the time of his 1952 entry, it is critical to determine whether his return from a few hours in Mexico in 1956 was an "entry" in the statutory sense. If it was not, the question whether Section 212 (a) (4) could constitutionally be applied to him need not be resolved.

98. 8 U.S.C. Section 1182 (a) (4) provides:

> Except as otherwise provided in this chapter, the following classes of aliens should be ineligible to receive visas and shall be excluded from admission into the United States:
> (4) Aliens afflicted with psychopathic personality, sexual deviation or a mental defect;

99. The United States Court of Appeals for the Ninth Circuit set aside the INS deportation order and enjoined its enforcement, holding that as applied to Fleuti Section 1182(a) (4) was unconstitutionally vague in that homosexuality was not sufficiently encompassed within the term "psychopathic personality." 302 F.2d 652 (1962).

100. 374 U.S. at 451.

101. *Id.* at 451–52.

102. 289 U.S. 422 (1933).

103. 374 U.S. at 453.

104. *Id.* at 453–57.

105. *Id.*

106. H.R. Rep. No. 1365, 82d Cong., 2d Sess. 32 (1952); S. Rep. No. 1137, 82d Cong., 2d Sess. 4 (1952).

107. 374 U.S. at 463.

108. *Id.*

109. *Supra* note 106.

110. 332 U.S. 388 (1947).

111. 158 F.2d 878 (2d Cir. 1947).

112. *See generally,* 374 U.S. at 463–67 (Harlan, J., dissenting).

113. *Id.* at 463 (Harlan, J., dissenting).

114. 443 U.S. 193 (1979).

115. *Id.* at 199.

116. Section 703 (a) of Title VII, 42 U.S.C. Section 2003–02(a) (1976) provides:

> (a) It shall be an unlawful employment practice for an employer
> (1) to fail or refuse to hire or to discharge any individual, or otherwise to discriminate against any individual with respect

to his compensation, terms, conditions or privileges of employment, because of such individual's race, color, religion, sex or national origin; or

(2) to limit, segregate, or classify his employees or applicants for employment in any way which would deprive or tend to deprive any individual of employment opportunities or otherwise adversely affect his status as an employee, because of such individual's race, color, religion, sex or national origin.

Section 703 (d) of Title VII, 42 U.S.C. Section 2000e–2(d) (1976), provides:

It shall be an unlawful employment practice for any employer, labor organization, or joint-management committee controlling apprenticeship or other training or retraining, including on-the-job training programs to discriminate against any individual because of his race, color, religion, sex, or national origin in admission to or employment in, any program established to provide apprenticeship or other training.

42 U.S.C. Section 2000e–2(j). The Section in full reads:

(j) Nothing contained in this subchapter shall be interpreted to require any employer, employment agency, labor organization, or joint labor-management committee subject to this subchapter to grant preferential treatment to any individual or to any group because of the race, color, religion, sex, or national origin of such individual or group on account of an imbalance which may exist with respect to the total number or percentage of persons of any race, color, religion, sex, or national origin employed by any employer, referred or classified for employment by any employment agency or labor organization, admitted to membership or classified by any labor organization, or admitted to, or employed in, any apprenticeship or other training program, in comparison with the total number or percentage of persons of such race, color, religion, sex, or national origin in any community, State, section, or other area, or in the available work force in any community, State, section, or other area.

117. 443 U.S. at 209.
118. *Id.* at 219 (Rehnquist, J., dissenting).
119. Abraham, *supra* note 18, at 384 (1980).
120. *Id.* at 384–85.
121. *Id.*

122. 443 U.S. at 202–03.

123. *See* Justice Rehnquist's documentation of these matters in 443 U.S. 222, n. 2 and 246 (Rehnquist, J., dissenting).

124. *Id.* at 222, n. 2.

125. *Id.* at 246.

126. 443 U.S. at 216 (Burger, C.J., dissenting).

127. 367 U.S. 643 (1961).

128. *Weeks v. United States,* 232 U.S. 383 (1914). *See also* Schlesinger, Exclusionary Injustice: The Problem of Illegally Obtained Evidence 14–18 (1977).

129. *See* Schlesinger, *id.* at 60–61.

130. 367 U.S. at 660.

131. *Id.* at 656.

132. *Id.* at 651. "There is language in Justice Clark's opinion which has convinced some readers that the decision was based upon the rule's deterrent effect, but the deterrent effect of the exclusionary rule was clearly only a factual consideration as opposed to a logical deduction from constitutional language." Schlesinger and Wilson, Property, Privacy and Deterrence: The Exclusionary Rule in Search of a Rationale, 18 Duq. L. Rev. 225, 235–37 (1980).

133. *Linkletter v. Walker,* 381 U.S. 618 (1965); *United States v. Calandra,* 414 U.S. 338 (1974).

134. *Linkletter,* 381 U.S. at 636–37. In *Calandra, id.,* Justice Powell writing for the majority asserted that the rule's prime purpose is to deter future unlawful police conduct and thereby effectuate the guarantee of the Fourth Amendment against unreasonable search and seizure. 414 U.S. at 347.

135. 367 U.S. at 652.

136. 428 U.S. 465 (1976).

137. Oaks, Studying the Exclusionary Rule in Search and Seizure, 37 U. Chi. L. Rev. 665 (1970); Ban, The Impact of *Mapp v. Ohio* on Police Behavior (delivered at the annual meeting of the Midwest Political Science Association, Chicago, May 1973); Ban, Local Courts v. the Supreme Court: The Impact of *Mapp v. Ohio* (delivered at the annual meeting of the American Political Science Association, New Orleans, 1973); Spiotto, Search and Seizure: An Empirical Study of the Exclusionary Rule and its Alternatives, 2 J. Legal Studies 243 (1973); Canon, Is the Exclusionary Rule in Failing Health? Some New Data and a Plea Against a Precipitous Conclusion, 62 Ky. L. J. 686 (1973–74); Canon, Testing the Effectiveness of Civil Liberties Policies at the

State and Local Levels: The Case of the Exclusionary Rule, 5 Am. Politics Q. 57 (1977); Effect of *Mapp v. Ohio* on Police Search and Seizure Practice in Narcotics Cases, 4 Col. L. J. and Soc. Prob. 87 (1968).

138. *Id.,* Canon, Is the Exclusionary Rule . . . ?

139. *Id.,* Canon, Testing the Effectiveness . . . , at 75.

140. *Id.,* Oaks, at 755.

141. *Id.*

142. *Id.*

143. For a further discussion of the material in this paragraph, *see* Schlesinger, *supra* n. 128 at 55–60.

144. 418 U.S. 323 (1974).

145. *Id.* at 341–43.

146. *Id.* at 349–50.

147. *Id.* at 350.

148. *Id.* at 347.

149. *Id.* at 400 (White, J., dissenting).

150. *Id.* at 394. *See* I. F. Harper and F. James, The Law of Torts § 5.29, p. 467 (1956); Note, Developments in the Law—Defamation, 69 Harv. L. Rev. 875, 938 and n. 443; and McCormick, Law of Damages, § 77, p. 278 for further discussion of limitations by judges and juries on libel awards.

151. *Id.*

152. Pedrick, Freedom of the Press and the Law of Libel: The Modern Revised Translation, 49 Corn. L. Q. 581, 587, fn. 23 (1964).

153. Sunderland, Trial by Jury, 11 U. Cinn. L. Rev. 120 (1927).

154. *Id.* at 122–28.

155. *See* Frank, Courts on Trial: Myth and Reality in American Justice, esp. chs. III and X (1949).

156. For a discussion of the problem of "perspectivity" and related matters, *see* Strauss, Natural Right and History, chs. 1 and 2 (1953).

157. Hamilton, Madison, and Jay, The Federalist, No. 78, 399 (ed. M. Beloff 1948).

158. 369 U.S. 186, 301–02 (1962) (Frankfurter, J., dissenting).

159. 367 U.S. 643, 682 (1961) (Harlan, J., dissenting).

160. *See* notes 15–18 *supra.*

161. Abraham, The Judicial Process 246 (1980).

162. Peltason, Federal Courts in the Political Process 27 (1955).

163. Schubert, Judicial Policy Making: The Political Role of the Courts 150 (1974).

164. Abraham, *supra* note 161 at 247.

165. Newland, Legal Periodicals and the United States Supreme Court, 3 Midwest Journal of Political Science 58 (1959).

166. *Id.* at 64.

167. 304 U.S. 64 (1938).

168. Warren, New Light on the History of the Federal Judiciary Act of 1789, 37 Harv. L. Rev. 49 (1923).

169. 16 Pet. 1 (1842).

170. 307 U.S. 277 (1939).

171. Newland, *supra* note 165, at 68–9.

172. *Id.* at 69.

173. 295 U.S. 422 (1935).

174. Newland, *supra* note 165, at 72.

175. For example, Professor Byrn says: "It is evident that the Court's finding that unborn children are not fourteenth amendment persons was deeply influenced by its own interpretation of history, which, for all practical purposes, was dictated by an uncritical acceptance of two law review articles by abortion advocate Cyril Means." Byrn, *supra* note 65, at 814. These articles are: Means, The Phoenix of Abortional Freedom: Is a Penumbral or Ninth-Amendment Right About to Arise from the Nineteenth-Century Legislative Ashes of a Fourteenth-Century Common-Law Liberty? 17 N.Y.L.F. 335 (1971) and Means, The Law of New York Concerning Abortion and the Status of the Foetus, 1664–1968: A Case of Cessation of Constitutionality, 14 N.Y.L.F. 411 (1968). *Id.* at note 63.

176. Yankelovich, Skelly and White, Inc., The Public Image of Courts: Highlights of a National Survey of the General Public, Judges, Lawyers and Community Leaders, prepared for the National Center for State Courts, 1978.

177. *Id.* at III.

178. *Id.* at II and III.

179. Ericson, Newspaper Coverage of the Supreme Court: A Case Study, 9 Journalism Quarterly 605, 607 (1977).

180. *Id.* at 606–07.

181. A Letter From the Presidents of the American Bar Association, the American Law Institute, the Association of American Law Schools, and the American Newspaper Publishers Association Foundation, found at 102, No. 1, S. Ct. back cover (1981).

182. *See* U.S.C. Canon 3A and resolution 6 for the prohibition on television in federal trial courts and in the circuit appeals courts.

The Supreme Court rules forbid the televising (or any photography) of its public proceedings.

183. Bass, Television's Day in Court, *New York Times,* Sec. VI, February 15, 1981, 36, 46.

184. *Tennessee Valley Authority v. Hill,* 437 U.S. 153 (1978).

185. *See,* for example, S.J. Res. 19 (sponsored by Senator Helms); S.J. Res. 110 (sponsored by Senator Hatch); H.J. Res. 50 (sponsored by Representative Hyde).

186. *See,* for example, S. 1647 (sponsored by Senator East); S. 1743 (sponsored by Senator Helms); H.J. Res. 16 (sponsored by Representative Ashbrook).

187. *See,* for example, Hart, *supra* note 16; Federal Judicial Center Study Group, Report on the Caseload of the Supreme Court (1972); Rehnquist, The Supreme Court: Past and Present, 59 A.B.A.J. 361 (1973). Supreme Court Justice John Paul Stevens, in a speech to the American Judicature Society, said recently that the quality of the Court's work was being undermined by an increasingly heavy caseload, which he called a matter of "national concern." *Washington Post,* August 7, 1982, 3.

188. Federal Judicial Center Study Group, *id.;* Warren, Attacks Freund Study Group's Composition and Proposal, 59 A.B.A.J. 721 (1973); Brennan, The National Court of Appeals: Another Dissent, 40 U. Chi. L. Rev. (1973).

189. Hart, *supra* note 16, at 100.

190. Barron and Miller, The Supreme Court, the Adversary System, and the Flow of Information to the Justices: A Preliminary Inquiry, 61 Va. L. Rev. 1187, 1233–40 (1975).

191. *Id.* at 1234.

192. *Id.*

193. Davis, Facts in Lawmaking, 80 Col. L. Rev. 930, 941 (1980).

194. *Id.* at 941–42.

195. Miller and Barron, *supra* note 190, at 1243–44.

196. *Id.* at 1244.

197. Quoted in Lewis, Gideon's Trumpet 164 (1964).

About the Author

Steven R. Schlesinger is Associate Chairman and Associate Professor in the Department of Politics at The Catholic University of America; he was previously a faculty member at Rutgers University. He received his B.A. degree from Cornell University (*cum laude* and with distinction in all subjects) and his M.A. and Ph.D. degrees from Claremont Graduate School. He is the author of *Federalism and Criminal Justice: The Case of the Exclusionary Rule* (1975) and of *Exclusionary Injustice: The Problem of Illegally Obtained Evidence* (1977); he is the editor of *Venue at the Crossroads* (1982). Professor Schlesinger has also written more than twenty articles in professional journals and has contributed chapters to a number of edited volumes. He was Adjunct Scholar at the National Legal Center for the Public Interest (Washington, D.C.) and is a consultant to the minority of the Constitution Subcommittee of the Senate Judiciary Committee as well as an instructor in the Intergovernmental Training Program of the Office of Personnel Management. He has received fellowships or research support from Rutgers University, the National Legal Center for the Public Interest, the Earhart Foundation, and the John M. Olin Foundation.

Professor Schlesinger is Acting Director of the Bureau of Justice Statistics in the U.S. Department of Justice.